OWEN McCAFFERTY

Born in 1961, Owen lives with his wife and three children in Belfast. His work includes *Mojo Mickybo* (Kabosh, Belfast, 1998); *No Place Like Home* (Tinderbox, Belfast, 2001); *Closing Time* (National Theatre, 2002); and *Scenes from the Big Picture*, also for the National Theatre.

Owen McCafferty

SHOOT THE CROW

NICK HERN BOOKS
London
www.nickhernbooks.co.uk

A Nick Hern Book

Shoot the Crow first published in Great Britain in 2003
as a paperback original by Nick Hern Books Limited,
14 Larden Road, London W3 7ST. Reprinted 2005

Typeset by Country Setting, Kingsdown, Kent CT14 8ES
Printed in Great Britain by CLE Print Ltd, St Ives PE27 3LE

ISBN-13   978 1 85459 726 7
ISBN-10   1 85459 726 4

A CIP catalogue record for this book is available from
the British Library

Shoot the Crow received its British premiere at the Royal
Exchange Theatre, Manchester, on 12 February 2003.
The cast was as follows:

SOCRATES	Patrick O'Kane
PETESY	Conleth Hill
DING-DING	Walter McMonagle
RANDOLPH	Paul Dinnen

Director   Jacob Murray
Designer   Laurie Dennett
Lighting Designer   Mark Distin
Sound Designer   Gwen Thompson

The play was originally staged on 26 February 1997 by the
Druid Theatre Company, Galway. The cast was as follows:

SOCRATES	David Ganley
PETESY	Anthony Brophy
DING-DING	Patrick Waldron
RANDOLPH	Fergal McElherran

Director   David Parnell
Designer   Paul McCavley
Lighting Designer   Tina MacHugh

The play was revived at the Trafalgar Studios, London, on
11 October 2005. The cast was as follows:

SOCRATES	James Nesbitt
PETESY	Conleth Hill
DING-DING	Jim Norton
RANDOLPH	Packy Lee

Director   Robert Delamere
Designer   Simon Higlett
Lighting Designer   Chris Davey

6

Characters

DING-DING, *sixty-five years old*

SOCRATES, *thirty-nine years old*

PETESY, *thirty-six years old*

RANDOLPH, *nineteen years old*

*The play takes place during the working day of four tilers on
a building site in Belfast. They are tiling adjoining rooms –
a public toilet and a shower area. The stage is divided in two.
There is a door leading to 'on-site'– ie, off stage – and
another between the two rooms. It is Friday, the end of the
working week.*

Mid-morning tea break. DING-DING *is asleep.* RANDOLPH
enters from on site carrying two cups of tea and a magazine.

RANDOLPH. petesy an socrates are stayin down in the other
    room – talkin a lotta shite – here's yer tea – don't mind me
    now – just you have a wee kip there an i'll run about like a
    blue arsed fly gettin you fuckin tea – tea in the special cup –
    (*He sets the cup down and circles it.*) – don't touch the cup –
    ding-ding's special cup – the cup – fuck you an yer cup –
    have a kip aye just you welt away there we'll all work roun
    ye – who needs cups when ya have bikin magazines that's
    what i say – (*He sits and opens his magazine.*) vroom
    fuckin vroom (DING-DING *wakes.*) look at that – a large
    set a wheels with some wee doll wrapped roun ye – is that
    the business or what – i get the readies t'gether that's me on
    the bike an off ski – long y'reckon it take t'do that – save
    for a bike – did a tell ye that's what i'm doin savin for a
    bike – long? – couldn't take that long like – a few squid
    every week – a few squid – join a club an that – have 'm –
    like christmas clubs only for motor bikes – long d'ya
    reckon? – need a licence first like – that'll not be a problem –
    me an ma mate been practisin on push bikes – same type a
    crack like innit – not as heavy or as fast but it's the same
    neck a the woods like – cuppla a shillins every week –
    licence – bike – an then it's the get yer philias fogg gear on
    ye an away we go – except i'd have some wee doll with me
    instead a that dopey french geezer he has knockin about
    with him – plus i'd be on a bike all the time instead a that
    trains steamers an balloon chats – wanna see the ones in the
    magazine i have – magic – wanna see the wee dolls innit
    fuckin unbelievable – big three wheel efforts – just lie back
    an sally on – big money they are like – big readies – take
    more than a few quid there every week – a wee one do me –
    so long as y'can fit two on it – go through that tunnel dixie
    a cuppla hours it's all pernod and distilled water an bung us
    another clatter a them frogs legs – a wee doll on the back a

the bike wingin yer way through france – an yous boys
fucked – slappin shit coloured tiles on some wee oul doll's
wall – d'ya reckon that ding-ding – what d'ya reckon

DING-DING. ya know fuck all – y'know that – fuck all about
fuck all

RANDOLPH. i'll be whistlin dixie with the camels roun the
kazbah – no sweat about it – vroom vroom

DING-DING. aye vroom vroom

RANDOLPH. aye – what – i've just told ye what i'm gonna do
regardin me an the world an the big picture – what's the
problem here – ya have t'make plans don't ye – isn't that
what we're all about – makin plans an that – gettin the stuff
ahead a ye sorted out

DING-DING. make plans – what for?

RANDOLPH. what for – what does that mean what for – the
future – that's the crack – ya do shit now so ya can sort
yerself out for the future – there's no point in graftin an that
if it's not gonna help ye paddle yer own dixie later in life is
there

DING-DING. that right – what's that?

RANDOLPH. what d'ya mean what is it it's a letter – a letter

DING-DING. correct a letter – who's it from?

RANDOLPH. c'mon til

DING-DING. heavy hole – it's a letter from heavy hole –
fucker

RANDOLPH. didn't send me one

DING-DING. no he didn't send you one – it's a thank you
letter – not typed now hand written – the personal touch –
he's thankin me for my time – doesn't say that but that's
what it means – the time i spent helpin him t'get wherever
he's goin – fuck'im – a lifetime spent graftin an ya end up
with a thank you note – hand written – we mustn't forget
that – today's the day randolph kid – today's the day

RANDOLPH. thought ya weren't retirin til next week

DING-DING. no – today

RANDOLPH. did he drop ye anythin – sort ya out for a few extra squid

DING-DING. ya only get what's comin t'ye in this world son – in my case that adds up t'fuck all squared

RANDOLPH. fuck'im

DING-DING. correct fuck'im

RANDOLPH. no more graftin for ye – yer home on a boat that way – feet up in front a the dixie – few bets eye the gee gees cuppla swallys in the afternoon – fuckin landed ya are

DING-DING. that's what a mean randolph son – that's what i'm tellin ye – ya know fuck all about fuck all – see that letter – that's what all yer plans amount til – fuck all

RANDOLPH. a few quid away a week – i know what am at – i'll not be hangin aroun for any fuckin letter from some geezer who wouldn't recognise yer coupin if he passed ye in the street – fuck at

DING-DING. go now – do it now – see if ya don't yer goose an ducked – longer ya spend doin this tighter the noose gets round yer fuckin neck – an after a while it's you that tightens it cause ye get used to the feel a the rope – do it now – get the bike now an go now

RANDOLPH. what with – a need t'earn some readies t'get it don't a

DING-DING. fuckin steal it if ya have to – do whatever ya have t'do – all i'm sayin is don't let fuck all pass ya by – thinkin about somethin unless ya do it does nothin but fuck ye up

RANDOLPH. a work – a earn readies – a get the bike – that's it there's nothin else to it – simple

DING-DING. work – work – ya know what work is – it's a fuckin con – work lets ye think ya can sprint like a gazelle then it straps fuckin lead boots roun yer plates a meat – i've a few shillins in ma sky rocket look at me i'm a king – only problems is son the few shillins is never enough to buy yerself a fuckin crown – ya always think the crowns on the cards though – it must be other people wear them – until one day yer standin in some shit hole talkin t'some kid with a hand written letter in yer pocket sayin thank you for yer trouble – it's a fuckin con – an know what the real beauty about all that is – the real sting in the tail – ya can't do without it – cause if ya don't have it yer napper goes – no work an the head's away

RANDOLPH. stop givin me grief ding-ding will ye

DING-DING. i'm tryin t'help ye here – what is it the bike means t'ye – escape – freedom – gettin t'fuck out – doin yer own thing bein yer own man – that what it means – i'll help ye get it

RANDOLPH. you a big sackfull a readies planked somewhere aye

DING-DING. there's a pallet a tiles lyin roun the front there right

RANDOLPH. aye

DING-DING. we'll steal them

RANDOLPH. get t'fuck – what an get nathered like that plumber fella the other day

DING-DING. fuck him

RANDOLPH. nothin t'do with him – it's t'do with gettin caught

DING-DING. ya want the bike don't ye – this is a way a gettin – it the only way a gettin it – i'll help ye out

RANDOLPH. how you helpin me out i didn't suggest it – helpin yerself out – gettin back at heavy hole or somethin

DING-DING. fuck all t'do with heavy hole

RANDOLPH. what?

DING-DING. what what?

RANDOLPH. what's in it for you besides that deep inner feelin of warmth ya get from helpin a work mate – that ya didn't much give a fuck about before

DING-DING. d'ya want it or don't ye?

RANDOLPH. what do you want?

DING-DING. same as you

RANDOLPH. what's that?

DING-DING. not t'be trapped – not t'wake up in the mornin an wish ya had some other punter's life cause yer's isn't the shit ya thought it was cracked up t'be

RANDOLPH. after t'day you can do that can't ye – no pressure on ye – do whatever ya want – ye've time t'do that now – isn't that what it's all about retirin an that – time t'ease off or whatever

DING-DING. a don't want time that's the fuckin point – time's no good to ye when ye've been used t'not havin any – it fucks ya up – a don't want that

RANDOLPH. what then – what?

DING-DING. a winda cleaner – i'm gonna be a winda cleaner

RANDOLPH. get t'fuck – winda cleaner – aye winda cleaner – a know aye

DING-DING. somethin wrong with that – it's not gonna make me rockafella but it'll get me a few shillins every week an give me somethin t'do – that's all i'm lookin a few shillins an somethin t'do

RANDOLPH. yer gonna steal like so ya can be a winda cleaner

DING-DING. correct

RANDOLPH. this might seem like an obvious question to you ding-ding – cause at the moment ya seem t'be workin on a different type of a fuckin level from the rest of us – but why do ya need a chunk a readies in order t'become a fuckin winda cleaner – ya gonna buy a gold plated bucket aye

DING-DING. a have t'buy somebody else's roun off them
    that's why – a was panickin about this retirement chat then
    somethin happened an i thought that'll do me – there's this
    oul lad lives two doors down from me – oul lad – that's
    fuckin good – fella's only two years older than me – he's a
    winda cleaner – cuppla weeks back he couped off the ladder
    an fucked his leg up – can't clean windas no more – i met
    him limpin his way roun for a few pints – sittin with other
    fuckers like himself all hatin each other for bein there – i'm
    talkin to him he's tellin me about his leg an that – i kept
    thinkin t'myself he's fucked – ya could see it in his lamps –
    dead – empty – no fuckin spark in them y'know – nothin
    t'fill his time with ya see – his napper's gone he's fucked –
    that can't happen t'me randolph son – they'll find that oul
    lad in six months' time sittin in his chair stiff as a board –
    cold as ice – dead for four days an no fucker know about it –
    that's not on randolph kid – that's no way for any human
    t'end up – he's sellin his roun – first come first served – if
    i get in there now i'm in business

RANDOLPH. i don't get that – that doesn't make any sense
    t'me – somethin ye like doin aye – a can understan that –
    but where's the pleasure in standin half way up a ladder –
    wet – monkeys – wipin the suds of some fucker's window –
    a don't get that – the thinkin behind that's all up the left

DING-DING. fuck all that – what i'm doin has got fuck all
    t'do with you right – this is about you – you want readies
    towards yer bikin fund – well this is an opportunity – that's
    all you gotta concern yerself with – fuck all else

RANDOLPH. what about petesy an socrates – say anythin
    t'them – what about them?

DING-DING. just me an you – nothin t'do with them it's just
    me an you

RANDOLPH. say fuck all

DING-DING. say fuck all – between me an you – nobody
    else's business

RANDOLPH. they were involved ya'd have t'split it four ways
    then wouldn't ye

DING-DING. ya would

RANDOLPH. fuck that

DING-DING. half better than a quarter

RANDOLPH. ya got all the gear then?

DING-DING. what gear?

RANDOLPH. the black gear – ya got all the black gear?

DING-DING. black gear?

RANDOLPH. tights – jumpers – gloves – those woolly chats
     ya pull over yer napper

DING-DING. ropes an pulleys

RANDOLPH. aye

DING-DING. helicopter be handy

RANDOLPH. helicopter?

DING-DING. we're shiftin tiles into a van at lunch time we're
     not stormin the fuckin embassy

RANDOLPH. lunchtime – lunchtime?– that's fuckin daylight
     that is

DING-DING. correct – we'll not need fuckin torches then
     either will wa – place is empty at lunch time – no hassle –
     fire the tiles in til the van – shift them plank them – get
     back t'them later

RANDOLPH. that all like – nothin else no?

DING-DING. what?

RANDOLPH. i don't know – just seems very normal like –
     very ordinary or somethin

DING-DING. we're just stealin tiles randolph son – if tilers are
     gonna steal somethin tiles seems like the obvious thing
     y'know – if we worked down a diamond mine now that be
     a different matter – but things bein what they are we're
     stuck with the fuckin tiles

RANDOLPH. talk me through it again

DING-DING. a just fuckin said

RANDOLPH. talk me through it

DING-DING. lunch – tiles – van – shift – plank – sell – bingo

RANDOLPH. not need masks then?

DING-DING. don't fuck me about boy

RANDOLPH. a wanna wear a mask – i want it t'be at night –
cut the fence gear with them big clunky scissors – drug the
guard dogs with meat an pills an shit – a robbery y'know
like a real robbery – pity a didn't have the bike – quick get
away – off ski

DING-DING *grabs* RANDOLPH *by the throat.*

DING-DING. this isn't a joke – i can't have ya fuckin things
up for me y'understand – ya can't fuck things up

RANDOLPH. yer hurtin me

DING-DING. either yer doin it or yer not – but don't think ya
can fuckin mess me about on this

RANDOLPH. i'm not

DING-DING *lets go.*

DING-DING. if ya don't wanna do it just say so – if you want
somethin badly enough ya take risks to get it – do you want
it or don't ye?

RANDOLPH. a don't know – what do you think – i don't know

DING-DING. i'm not tellin ye what t'do ya make yer own
decisions – know yer own mind an do what ye think's best

RANDOLPH. if we're caught i'm fucked

DING-DING. an if we're not

RANDOLPH. if we're not i'm half way there

DING-DING. vroom vroom – randolph – vroom vroom

RANDOLPH. lunchtime

DING-DING. lunchtime

SOCRATES *and* PETESY *enter other room from on site.*

PETESY. if it's not in the other room it has t'be here – or there

SOCRATES. aye whatever – do ya understan what i'm sayin about this – it's like ya were on a journey an yer lookin at the scenery an shit as ye go along – then ya arrive where yer meant t'be at – but if somebody was to say t'ye what road did ye take – how'd ye get here – ya wouldn't be able t'fuckin say – that's the type a thing i'm talkin about – understan what i'm sayin?

PETESY. you have a look for it i'll check on these two

SOCRATES. yer not listenin t'me

PETESY. just have a jeff juke about the place will ye

SOCRATES. aye

PETESY (*enters other room*). he's doin my fuckin napper in again

DING-DING. his head's gone

PETESY. we're on journeys now that have no roads or somethin – doin my fuckin napper in – come in t'do a day's graft – ya end up slappin on tiles with one a them fuckin tibetan chats that sit on their jam roll an do their nappers in with thinkin

DING-DING. his head's gone

PETESY. aye

DING-DING. aye

PETESY. what's the crack in here ya's weltin away at this or what

DING-DING. finished up there aye

PETESY. bit a groutin just – have t'be red up t'day now

DING-DING. aye

PETESY. ya gettin plenty a work outta him ding-ding aye

RANDOLPH. i'm alright

PETESY. just you keep cleanin the buckets – never enough clean buckets – always need clean buckets ding-ding don't ye

DING-DING. oh aye – clean buckets

PETESY. got one dipped in bronze do ye for yer retirement chat

DING-DING. aye

PETESY. no more graftin – pig in shit wha

DING-DING. aye

PETESY. aye – yous two see a delivery note lyin about no?

DING-DING. what ya want it for?

PETESY. check the adhesive on the job

DING-DING. nah

PETESY. if he's nothin t'do ding-ding fire him in with us

DING-DING. aye

RANDOLPH. plenty t'do

PETESY. day's work kill ye

RANDOLPH. aye a know

PETESY. away back in here t'talk to the oracle

DING-DING. his head's away

> PETESY *exits next door.* RANDOLPH *makes masturbatory gestures after him.*

PETESY. two tossers – ya find that?

SOCRATES. wha

PETESY. what d'ya mean what – a said to ye have a butcher's for the deliver note

SOCRATES. fuck the delivery note

PETESY. it's important a wanna see if these tiles are on it or not

SOCRATES. fuck the tiles

PETESY. fuck the delivery note – fuck the tiles – we'll all just sit here with our heads jammed up our onion will wa

SOCRATES. delivery note – that it like – that where we are – aye

PETESY. yes

SOCRATES. i'm tryin t'make sense of somethin here – understan what i'm sayin – i'm tryin to throw a curve ball – have a look at things from a different dixie – a different perspective – know what a mean

PETESY (*looking for delivery note*). no

SOCRATES. tilt the beam of light that's fuckin dixin down on us at a different angle y'know

PETESY. aye

SOCRATES. i'm standin at a bus stop other mornin – monday mornin early – this guy a know from when a was a kid stanin across the way – there's two winos waitin t'get their starter for the day – he queues up with them – i'm thinkin he's goin in for a packet a smokes on his way t'work – he's a plumber or somethin fucked like that – the place opens an the three a them are like greyhounds out a the trap – he didn't get smokes he bought a carry out – couldn't even be bothered fuckin puttin it in a bag – four tins a that rocket fuel gear in his hand – doesn't give a fuck who sees him cause his head's fixed on the gargle – i used t'kick football with this guy now he's millin four tins of piss yer begs gear t'wake him up – t'get him sorted out – it frightened me y'know – lookin at him fucked me up

PETESY. some fella ya played headers with turned into a wino – what?

SOCRATES. what happened t'that guy – how'd he arrive where he's at – what happened between bein a kid an doin all that shit and millin tins up an entry on a fuckin monday morning – what happened?

PETESY. ya gonna help me look for this?

SOCRATES. know what a realised when a was lookin at this guy – he had his own life – i still thought of him as the wee lad kickin football – but he wasn't – he was there living out his own life – that meant i was living out my life but i'd never fuckin noticed that before – know what i'm sayin – i wasn't aware of my own life

PETESY. look under the tool box

SOCRATES. fuck the delivery note – i'm not interested

PETESY. look under the tool box

SOCRATES. fuck the delivery note – fuck the box – if yer not aware of yer own life it means that ye haven't really participated in the shit that happens t'ye – so ya end up at a certain point thinkin how the fuck did i get here – like there was no control over it y'know – i'm doin this i'm doin that – i'm separated – i haven't seen her and the wee lad for a cuppla months – what's all that about – how'd that happen – was it always gonna happen – could i have stopped it from happenin – what does shit like that mean?

PETESY. i can't find it – no delivery note – the tiles don't exist – happy days

SOCRATES. what d'ya reckon – it's like do we live our own lives or do we live them through other people or what – what d'ya think?

PETESY. don't know – the don't exist – a told ye – nobody knows about them – didn't a tell ya that

SOCRATES. are ya listenin t'me – d'ya have any thoughts on shit like this – is it just me or we all like that or what – what d'ya think?

PETESY. socrates stop it – just fuckin stop it – i have no room for this gear y'understan – i've other stuff in my life t'sort out – practical shit y'know – the real world – mortgages – bills – work – that world – understand – the don't exist – right – all we gotta do is fire them in the van

SOCRATES. so that's it – nothin else – that's it – all we're about is stealing tiles is it

PETESY. correct a mundo – twenty minutes gets them in the van nobody's any the wiser

SOCRATES. the real world the – practical world

PETESY. real – practical – yes

SOCRATES. one a the plumbers got caught tea leafin the other day – he's banjaxed – that practical enough

PETESY. an what?

SOCRATES. he's out – we get caught we're out

PETESY. a heard nothin about that – what plumber?

SOCRATES. what plumber – what plumber – the plumber plumber

PETESY. there's two plumbers

SOCRATES. the big fat geezer

PETESY. they're both big fat geezers

SOCRATES. the one that kicked a hole in an alsation's throat – that one

PETESY. a doberman – an the fella ripped its lugs off

SOCRATES. ripped its lugs off? – what for – you talk a lotta balls y'know that

PETESY. wasn't it goin after one of his kids or somethin – another thing too it was a spark not a plumber – know the wee small one with the big napper an the goat beard – him

SOCRATES. him – sure he's not married

PETESY. maybe the dog was goin for him then i don't know

SOCRATES. what would he rip the ears off it for?

PETESY. to fuckin stop it

SOCRATES. how would that stop it?

PETESY. rippin its lugs off wouldn't stop it?

SOCRATES. no – that just piss the dog off – kickin a hole in its throat's a different matter – can't do any damage if it's a chelsea boot stuck in its throat

PETESY. oh – neither of the plumbers wear chelsea boots –
the spark does though

SOCRATES. that's not right now cause they all wear trainers –
in case they get a shock

PETESY. ya couldn't kick a hole in a dog's throat if ya were
wearin trainers anyway

SOCRATES. why not?

PETESY. why not – what's wrong with you why not – cause
they're made for runnin not kickin holes in the throats of
mad fuckin dogs

SOCRATES. chelsea boots are – are the

PETESY. well there's certainly a bit more fuckin wear an tear
in them isn't there

SOCRATES. kicked a hole in yer head

PETESY. doberman – no ears – spark

SOCRATES. whatever – fuck that – the fat plumber one with
the beard

PETESY. him aye

SOCRATES. banjaxed

PETESY. what's that gotta do with us

SOCRATES. heavy hole'll be on the look out now

PETESY. no delivery note – so the don't exist

SOCRATES. they're not ours know what a mean – the don't
belong t'us

PETESY. things that you tea leaf don't normally belong to you
else there'd be no point in fuckin stealing them

SOCRATES. aye but we know heavy hole – we know him –
that makes it personal

PETESY. fuck heavy hole – what's he ever done for us?

SOCRATES. that's not the point

PETESY. that's precisely the point – he ever invite ye up til his house – no – ya ever go out for a swally with him – no – you on his christmas card list – fuckin no – we don't know him he employs us that's it – he's a businessman an we graft for him – fuck all personal about that

SOCRATES. what that mean we're entitled to steal off him?

PETESY. accordin to the rules i live by yes – he's a lot more than i'll ever have an i helped him get it so fuck'im

SOCRATES. aye a know fuck'im – but ya know what a mean – there's a principle involved here – like it or not he's part of our world isn't he – it be like stealin from yer own – morally it's not right

PETESY. tell me this well – is it morally right that we only get paid enough readies – on purpose by the way don't forget that on purpose – that we only get paid enough readies t'keep our heads a cuppla inches above the shit heap – is that morally right?

SOCRATES. ya get paid the worth of what ya do – fuckin market forces an all that gear dictate that don't the – that's fuck all to do with heavy hole – economics – supply an demand – that's what that's all about

PETESY. look all them things are a con – they're there t'make sure that people who haven't a pot t'piss in remain without a pot t'piss in – i don't go by those rules – i go by rules that suit me not someone else

SOCRATES. it's difficult isn't it – makin up yer mind about stuff – havin problems about decidin about things at the moment y'know

PETESY. it's not life an death shit socrates we're only stealin a pallet of fuckin tiles – look – heavy hole's insured we steal the tiles he claims the readies back – what's fairer than that?

SOCRATES. that's true now – hadn't thought about that one – that illuminates the whole proceedins a touch – what about the other two?

PETESY. fuck'em

SOCRATES. fuck'em?

PETESY. nothin t'do with them – they're t'know nothin about it – it's between me an you

SOCRATES. just me an you

PETESY. just me an you – sixty-forty split

SOCRATES. sixty-forty?

PETESY. aye – i get the biggest share cause it was my idea

SOCRATES. how d'ya know i wasn't thinkin about it

PETESY. didn't ya just give me all that right an wrong shite

SOCRATES. might've been lyin – could've been thinkin about it all along

PETESY. ya said fuck all well

SOCRATES. a wanted t'see how the land lay – what yer tellin me here is you get extra readies for speakin

PETESY. how the fuckin land lay – right – alright – were ya thinkin about it?

SOCRATES. no

PETESY. what the fuck then

SOCRATES. sixty forty – if we're caught aren't we both goose an ducked – so what's this sixty-forty business

PETESY. just for the sake of argument ya were thinkin about it – ya didn't give it any of the verbals so there's no point in it – i thought it and spoke it – so i started the whole process off – that's why sixty-forty – anyway it's me that has the contacts

SOCRATES. who?

PETESY. if a tell ye you'll know then

SOCRATES. correct – who?

PETESY. jimmy blow

SOCRATES. jimmy blow – jimmy fuckin blow – the whole site knows that

PETESY. aye but ya said fuck all – it's the same thing

SOCRATES. sixty forty behave yerself (DING-DING *enters from the other room.*) that's not on y'know

PETESY. alright in there ding-ding aye

DING-DING. aye – need another pair a snips spring's gone in mine

PETESY. in the tool box

SOCRATES. sixty fuckin forty

PETESY. sixty forty listen t'him will ye – we're tryin t'work out ding-ding – what the percentage split would be between – fruit an sugar in a pot a jam – i reckon sixty forty

DING-DING. sounds right to me

SOCRATES. it's not well – i'm tellin ye it's not

PETESY. aye – ya get the snips ding-ding?

DING-DING. aye – find the deliver note did ye?

PETESY. no – doesn't matter i'll count the buckets or somethin

DING-DING. if ya come across it give us a shout

PETESY. what for?

DING-DING. i wanna check somethin on it

PETESY. check what?

DING-DING. somethin

PETESY. aye but what?

DING-DING. nothin

PETESY. somethin – nothin – what?

DING-DING. a think we're a box a spacers short – if a had the note a could check it y'know

PETESY. if a come across it sure i'll fire it in t'ye

DING-DING. aye – sixty forty sounds right t'me socrates

SOCRATES. not in my book it's not

PETESY. cook book ding-ding wha

> DING-DING *exits to other room.*

PETESY. what's wrong with you – they're not t'know nothin about this – say nothin

SOCRATES. a don't know about all this

PETESY. ya can't back out now it's all up an runnin

SOCRATES. i didn't declare my hand either way – we're just talkin – all we're doin is talkin

PETESY. a can't do it on my swanny it's a two man effort

SOCRATES. a fifty fifty effort

PETESY. puttin me under pressure now

SOCRATES. i'm just sayin what's fair that's all

PETESY. what's fair

SOCRATES. aye

PETESY. scrub it – forget it – we'll not do it that's fair

SOCRATES. aye

PETESY. aye

SOCRATES. you positive now – it's clear it's sorted out in yer head – the war's over regardin this

PETESY. not doin it

SOCRATES. i've a suggestion well

PETESY. what?

SOCRATES. see the pallet a tiles out there nobody knows about we'll steal them

PETESY. away an fuck

SOCRATES. if we agree t'steal them i get a bigger whack cause it was my idea

PETESY. my idea

SOCRATES. that was a different idea which you've just knocked on the head – this is a new idea – my idea

PETESY. who's yer contact

SOCRATES. jimmy blow

PETESY. fuck off

SOCRATES. my idea – my contact – what's the problem

PETESY. i need the readies

SOCRATES. who am i the fuckin aga khan

PETESY. a need it for somethin definite – it has t'be got – everythin else is shit right forget about all that this is the reason right

SOCRATES. what – what is it?

PETESY. ya gonna let me explain – this is personal shit a don't like doin this – i'm forcin myself t'tell ye y'know

SOCRATES. welt away

PETESY. thank you

SOCRATES. it's a pleasure

PETESY. one a the kids – the eldest wee girl – really bright kid y'know – fuckin frighten ye sometimes the crack she comes off with – intellectual gear i have problems gettin my head round y'know – me an her ma sittin there half the time with blank coupons just listenin til her – she's top trick in school an all that business – anyway her school's doing this exchange dixie extended holiday type a thing t'france – an she's been picked to go – there's grant money available from somewhere – which is fine – but you've gotta fork out a big whack of it yerself – the readies has t'be in next week – haven't got it understan – in a way i'm thinkin fuck it it's only a holiday she doesn't go it's not the end a the world for her – but in the back a my mind i keep thinkin this an opportunity for the kid – experience stuff i didn't experience – go t'places i've never been – somethin might come of it y'know – all this shit here it's good enough for me it's what i'm used to – but if somethin better can happen for her why shouldn't it happen – an even if it didn't it would be somethin to look back on y'know – that's it – that's the reason

SOCRATES. i don't believe you just told me that

PETESY. i didn't wanna say – didn't a say a didn't wanna say

SOCRATES. ya fuckin did though

PETESY. no sixty forty fifty fifty

SOCRATES. very good that's very good petesy

PETESY. what?

SOCRATES. i take any type a cut a look like a complete bastard now don't a

PETESY. are ya in or out?

SOCRATES. hobson's fuckin choice

PETESY. forget a told ye

SOCRATES. aye

PETESY. i'm serious forget about it – yer either in or out

SOCRATES. what if a say no – you be happy with that?

PETESY. ya say no ya say no – are ya sayin no?

SOCRATES. i'm not happy about this petesy – emotional fuckin blackmail y'know – i'm not happy about that – made me responsible for shit that i'm not responsible for

PETESY. responsible for fuck all – if ya don't wanna do it then don't do it – makin me feel like i'm beggin ye here – fuck off – my family i'll look after them – a don't need you or no other fucker – emotional blackmail – a business deal that's what yer bein offered – a fuckin business deal – don't think yer doin me any favours – it's a business deal an nothin else

SOCRATES. right alright sixty forty

PETESY. no fifty fifty i want fuck all from ye

SOCRATES. a don't mind if

PETESY. a don't give a fuck what ya mind – this is a business deal – fifty fifty or nothin

SOCRATES. don't be gettin all fuckin heavy here

PETESY. i'm not i'm calm – yes or no?

SOCRATES. alright

PETESY. ya sure now?

SOCRATES. d'ya want me t'sign somethin – i've said alright haven't a

PETESY. have t'be at lunch time

SOCRATES. aye

PETESY. just need t'get ridda them other two – say we'll meet them for a swally roun the corner – celebrate ding-ding's good night irene trick

SOCRATES. aye

PETESY. i take the wee lad roun now clean the van – get it ready

SOCRATES. aye

PETESY. everything sound?

SOCRATES. aye

PETESY. bit silent on it y'know

SOCRATES. i'm agreein with ye – aye means i'm agreein with ye

PETESY. you be alright here on yer own – get everythin squared up

SOCRATES. aye

PETESY. in the name of fuck (*Enters other room.*) you be alright on your todd ding-ding

DING-DING. aye

PETESY. c'mon randolph me an yous going to clean the van out

RANDOLPH. why?

PETESY. what does it matter to you why we're just doin it –
    so c'mon – fancy a cuppla gargles at lunchtime ding-ding –
    all head roun the corner bit of a celebration an that

DING-DING. lunch time

PETESY. aye

DING-DING. i've a cuppla things t'get sorted out

PETESY. yer last day y'know can't let it go without an oul
    swally an that

DING-DING. we'll see

PETESY. c'mon you

    PETESY *and* RANDOLPH *exit to on site.*

SOCRATES. no talk about nothin just words – no talk (*Makes
    an attempt to go back to work.*) I can't be arsed with all this
    (*He enters other room where* DING-DING *is working.*) ya
    busy?

DING-DING. enough t'keep me goin

SOCRATES. aye

    SOCRATES *sits down and watches* DING DING *work.*

DING-DING. ya finished in there?

SOCRATES. nah

DING-DING. much a do?

SOCRATES. nah

DING-DING. adhesive's shite – too dry – lyin too long

SOCRATES. d'ye ever cry ding-ding? – ye ever just sit down
    an cry?

DING-DING. no

SOCRATES. i did the other day – a worked somethin out for
    myself an cause a realised the truth about somethin it made
    me cry – it's like it had been there all along an it was slowly

workin its way out y'know – somethin locked inside me
waitin to be worked out – d'ya ever get that – ever feel like
there's shit locked away deep down or whatever tryin t'bust
out or somethin

DING-DING. no

SOCRATES. it was to do with my da – him as a person
y'know – d'ye ever do that – think about what type of
person yer da was really like y'know – get rid a all that
sentimental fuckin gear an just have a look – d'ya ever do
that?

DING-DING. no – give us over them snips

SOCRATES (*he does*). everybody thought my da was a great
fella y'know a character – yer da's a character – always
remember people sayin that – dead now like – yer brown
bread doesn't matter a fuck what ya were does it – yer oul
lad dead aye?

DING-DING. a lifetime – retirement fucked 'im

SOCRATES. my oul lad was a hero t'me – when i was a kid a
used t'think that if everybody respected me the way people
respected my da that yer life would be worthwhile y'know –
somethin worth livin – his funeral was fuckin massive – all
weepin – there'll not be another one like yer da – if yer
half the man yer da was you'll do alright son – ya never
understand shit that's goin on aroun ye til after it's over sure
ye don't – bright man never made anything of himself
y'know – spent all his life graftin – digging – liftin –
sweatin – that fucked him up – took to the gargle an that's
when everybody thought he was a great fella – on friday's
i had t'go roun t'the bar an get money off him for my ma
y'know – i can see him sittin there crowd round him drink
flyin an him holdin court – used to bring me into the middle
of them y'know – cause i was his son that made me a great
fella too – a hero my hero – y'know what i worked out
ding-ding – the thing that made me cry – i worked out that
there's difference between bein a character and havin
character – my da was a small insignificant little person who
gave a fuck about nobody but himself – he thought more

about gettin a slap on the back for bein a great fella by some other useless fucker than he did about the people that should've mattered to him – his family his wife his kids – when i was fifteen he fucked off – gave me some bullshit speech about how his life was a failure an how he was a burden on us all an then he fucked off – left me ma with five kids – still a character of course – still gettin the slaps on the back – no bottle – the man had no fuckin bottle – rather than live a decent life he wanted to be a character in a story – fuck'im

SOCRATES *cries, not openly but with resistance.* DING-DING *continues to work.* SOCRATES *stops crying. Silence.*

i'm sorry

DING-DING. aye

SOCRATES. i'm sorry ding-ding – i'm sorry

DING-DING. aye – that united's a bad lot aren't the – watched them the other night – gettin fuckin hammered the were end up winnin one t'nil – jammie bastards – other team must've hit the bar four times – wee lad rattled it from about thirty yards – like a fuckin bullet it was keeper didn't smell it – jammie bastards – ya see it – must've been thirty fuckin yards

SOCRATES. nah

DING-DING. good game – jammie bastards thirty yards like

SOCRATES. aye – things happen in cycles like don't the – same shit keeps comin roun again an again

DING-DING. that's right – same match last year same shit happened – jammie bastards

SOCRATES. a don't mean that – that's not what i'm talkin about – why the fuck would a wanna talk about that

DING-DING. what then?

SOCRATES. the same shit happens – my da fucks off – i end up fuckin off – a haven't seen her or my wee lad for months now – that's what i'm talkin about – that's what a mean

DING-DING. oh that – right

SOCRATES. aye that – not whether some pimply gobbed overpaid little runt can kick a fuckin ball or not – that – my life – that

DING-DING. aye

SOCRATES. a should go roun an see them shouldn't a – what d'ye think should i go round an see them?

DING-DING. i don't know – when?

SOCRATES. now – go roun an see them now – do it now

DING-DING. aye now – if it's in yer head do it now

SOCRATES. talk to them

DING-DING. aye talk to them – stay there for a while have lunch i'll cover for ye

SOCRATES. maybe arrange t'bring them out for dinner or somethin – bring them out t'night – just the three of us – talk to them

DING-DING. i'll cover for ye – dinner tonight's a good idea

SOCRATES. you say t'petesy – tell him – tell him i'll be back soon

DING-DING. never mind about that – fuck that i'll sort that out

SOCRATES. aye now – now'd be the best time

DING-DING. aye

SOCRATES *exits to on site.*

PETESY *and* RANDOLPH *enter from on site.*

PETESY (*to* RANDOLPH). start sortin out that crap in the corner (*To* DING-DING.) where's heart on his sleeve away – saw him beltin out the gate there

DING-DING. away roun t'see his fork an knife an wee lad

PETESY. ya serious?

DING-DING. his head's away – one minute he's slabberin
about his da or somethin next thing he's up an away –
somethin not right with him

PETESY. he say how long like – what – gonna be away long
or what?

DING-DING. he just up an scarpered – i don't know

PETESY. he said nothin?

DING-DING. somethin about lunch

PETESY. back before lunch?

DING-DING. gonna have lunch with them he said

PETESY. lunch when – lunch when we're havin lunch – lunch
then or lunch some other time?

DING-DING. lunch he said – fuck i don't know – ya eat lunch
at lunch time don't ye – talkin about dinner as well

PETESY. not lunch then dinner – is that what he said dinner?

DING-DING. both – must be hank marvin

PETESY. let me get this straight here – he's not comin back
that it?

DING-DING. look petesy i don't know his head's done – he's
talkin about his da then he's on about his fork an knife an
wee lad then he's talkin about meals then he's up an away

PETESY. fuck'im – said nothin like just away – fuck'im

DING-DING. there's somethin not right with him i'm tellin ye

PETESY. a know that

DING-DING. i'm graftin away he's spoutin some cleavers
in my ear about discoverin somethin about his da or
somethin – next thing he's gurnin away like a child – mad
man know what i'm sayin – name a fuck ya can't be at that
crack – that's not on – ya can't be at that

PETESY. a know that – a know that – fuck'im

DING-DING. all the years i've been graftin never witnessed
the like a that – i've seen men go through some serious shit

but a mean it never got outta order – just burst into tears – a don't know what the fuck he was expectin me t'do – not equipped t'handle that gear like am a

PETESY. who the fuck is – that's the problem too he's puttin it on to us – he should know better like shouldn't he

DING-DING. correct – know better that's right

PETESY. you listenin to this randolph – this is important listen to what's bein said here

RANDOLPH. what?

PETESY. when yer workin with other men right in a situation like this – see all the emotional shit that ya get elsewhere keep it til yerself – cause once ya start givin it the verbals yer napper goes – men yer workin with don't want that – always gotta keep the napper straight

DING-DING. fuckin embarrassin that's what it is – embarrassin other people yer are

PETESY. man's right – not only are ye fuckin about with the relationships between you an yer workmates yer embarrassin people as well – first rule of work – if it's not within the chat that we work within ye say fuck all – remember that – fuck all

RANDOLPH. got ye – fuck all

DING-DING. tried to steer him away from it too havin none of it he was – he's givin it the weepin trick i piped in with what ya think about the match the other night

PETESY. that's a good one – sound bet – football's always a sound bet

DING-DING. fucker let on he hadn't seen the match

PETESY. he had an opportunity – ya give him an opportunity

DING-DING. practically told me to shut up – fuckin head's gone

PETESY. a know that – see the one yer wee man hit from thirty yards – fuckin doosey

DING-DING. jammie bastards – a kept sayin that

RANDOLPH. same wee lad hit one like that the other week too

DING-DING. a saw it – fuckin belter

PETESY. hit them with both feet he can

DING-DING. if the put that wee lad up for sale ya couldn't buy him – some a them third world chats wouldn't have enough national fuckin income to pay for that wee lad

PETESY. he's good

DING-DING. star he is

PETESY. he's not comin back then – fuck'im

DING-DING. lunchtime – after lunch – i don't know

PETESY. just up an away – fuck'im – i'm away here

PETESY *exits to other room.*

RANDOLPH. i reckon ya get ten million for that wee lad – he'll not stay with them that type a readies floatin about – ya think he'll stay with them?

DING-DING. don't give a fuck what he does son – that's socrates away durin lunch – all we gotta do now is get rid of shit for brains there

RANDOLPH. aye

DING-DING. what was all that crack about cleanin the van out?

RANDOLPH. nothin just said it looked like a shit heap

DING-DING. save us doin it

RANDOLPH. i did do it

DING-DING. save me doin it

RANDOLPH. aye

PETESY (*other room – thinking aloud*). swannin off – no reason like – can't trust a man at that crack – can't say what he's thinkin – fuck that (*Pause.*) randolph mere a minute

RANDOLPH (*enters other room*). what?

PETESY. shut the door behind ye

RANDOLPH. what?

PETESY. that cryin trick fucked ding-ding up didn't it – he's alright ding-ding isn't he – soun man

RANDOLPH. aye

PETESY. i was just thinkin about somethin there – just between me an you now – ya understan that

RANDOLPH. aye

PETESY. that's good – socrates' a bit dodgy at the moment y'know – ya get the feelin from him he'd drop tools an do a bunk on ye if it suited him – that's not a good situation work wise an with ding-ding packin it in it's all a bit up in the air y'know – could get somebody else in for ding-ding but then we mightn't hit if off with the guy or whatever y'know – an that would fuck the whole show up – might be a better idea if you took over from ding-ding

RANDOLPH. ya serious – that'd be brilliant petesy – a need the extra readies y'know an that would help me

PETESY. slow down there tonto nothin's sorted yet – normally take two or three months but i could bend heavy hole's ear about it – maybe speed the thing up – tell him yer sound get him on yer side y'know – think that be a good idea – would ya be up to it ye reckon?

RANDOLPH. certainly no sweat about it petesy i'd be sound

PETESY. few extra shillins in yer sky rocket of course come the end a the week

RANDOLPH. that'd be great – i'm savin to buy a motorbike y'know – have t'put money away in a club an that y'know

PETESY. are ye – that's good – extra responsibilities as a said – bit of decision makin

RANDOLPH. i can handle that

PETESY. i think ya could

RANDOLPH. when ya gonna say t'heavy hole soon like –
next week or what – when ya sayin til him?

PETESY. that depends on you

RANDOLPH. what way?

PETESY. fuck all for fuck all – i do somethin for you you do
somethin for me

RANDOLPH. what – anything name it

PETESY. pallet a tiles lyin out the front there – a want ya
t'help me steal them

RANDOLPH. shit

PETESY. there's nothing to it kid – just fire them into the back
a the van at lunchtime – shift them – that's it

RANDOLPH. pallet a tiles roun the front – lunchtime

PETESY. aye – fuck all to it plus there's a few quid there for
ye

RANDOLPH. lunchtime

PETESY. friday lunchtime everyone fucks off – place til
ourselves – happy days – tell ding ding meet him roun the
bar for a swally – weigh in late

RANDOLPH. what if i knock ya back?

PETESY. ya gonna knock me back?

RANDOLPH. don't know

PETESY. put it like this – no good word to heavy hole plus
i can make life shit for ye y'know

RANDOLPH. it is already

PETESY. more shit then – i need ye t'do this for me

RANDOLPH. why?

PETESY. got fuck all to do with you why – y'understand –
nothin – all you need know is i need someone t'give me a
hand – that's all – workmates helpin each other out – isn't
that the way the world should be

RANDOLPH. aye work mates helpin each other out

PETESY. just look upon it as a business deal that works to both our benefits – you get what you want i get what i want – nobody's any the wiser no harm done

RANDOLPH. aye

PETESY. away back in there give him a hand – oul fucker probably sleepin by now

RANDOLPH. aye

PETESY. ya get nothin for nothin kid

RANDOLPH. aye

> RANDOLPH *enters other room.*

DING-DING. what shit for brains want?

RANDOLPH. nothin

DING-DING. nothin

RANDOLPH. aye nothin (*Pause.* RANDOLPH *starts scratching his arms.*) fuckin arms goin mad with itch

DING-DING. grout dust – drop a soap an water sort that out

RANDOLPH. it's not that

DING-DING. what?

RANDOLPH. a didn't want t'say anythin to ye about it (*His head starts to twitch.*) there's that away now too (*Scratching – twitching – his body jerks.*) the jerkin now – it only happens at certain times – it's stress related – first happened when we were kids just about t'raid an orky an this started – first the scratching then the other gear

DING-DING. i've heard of it – (*Scratching.*) it can be serious (*Twitching/jerking.*) has been know to stay with people for years

RANDOLPH. stop fuckin about

DING-DING. maybe it's contagious

RANDOLPH. the stress comes from a reaction to the notion of gettin caught – my lamps will start to swell up soon then a go temporarily blind

DING-DING (*stops*). nothin wrong with a bit a nerves randolph son

RANDOLPH. no joke

DING-DING. don't fuck me about – a told ye that

RANDOLPH (*stops*). we'll leave it til monday tiles still here then it's a bog cert they're nobody's

DING-DING. this job's finished today – i'm leavin today – we're doin it – today (*Arm around* RANDOLPH's *shoulder.*) think about the motorbike – ya see it – just you keep that picture in yer head

RANDOLPH. but ding-ding it's not

DING-DING (*pulls* RANDOLPH *close-tight*). a commitment been made – there's nothing else t'be said – (*Smiling.*) don't panic son – there's no need to panic

RANDOLPH. i'm not i'm not i'm sound – just havin a bit of a laugh y'know – just a bit of an oul laugh – ease the tension a bit ding-ding that's all – nothin t'worry about where i'm concerned

DING-DING. we're sound then

RANDOLPH. alright if i go for a dander for five minutes – just want t'walk about the place check everything's alright y'know

DING-DING. you do that you do that son

RANDOLPH *exits to on site.*

DING-DING. temporary fuckin blindness – wha

PETESY *working in one room* DING-DING *in the other.* SOCRATES *enters from on site to room* DING-DING *is in.*

SOCRATES. thank you for covering for me – you are a man of good character an outstanding and upstanding individual whose worth – like all real martyrs – will only be realised when you bite the big one and take your rightful place amongst the gods

DING-DING. i thought

SOCRATES. don't think do – the foundation of all human endeavour

SOCRATES *exits to other room.*

DING-DING. fuck him

PETESY. where the fuck where you?

SOCRATES. this another lover's tiff honey – not jealous were you

PETESY. where were ye?

SOCRATES. i had an idea – a thought – i acted on it and from that some good has burst onto the scene – now the world's a happier place

PETESY. happier fuckin place – aye – ding-ding's said ya were away for lunch – lunch that's what he told me – just up'ed an fucked off – that's what he said

SOCRATES. aren't a here now – had t'come back for the pilfering chats didn't a

PETESY. i was thinkin about that – it might be better if

SOCRATES. all systems are go – know what happened t'me there – something small but something good which makes it probably something big doesn't it

PETESY. socrates about the other – thing there's somethin

SOCRATES. howl on a minute this is important a need to speak this out y'know – i'd worked out y'see that my da didn't treat his kids an wife well – an it looked like i was goin that way – so a said fuck it i'm goin roun t'see them – bit iffy at the start – so a thought i'll be honest here fuck it – i'll be honest – i'm confused i said – i'm lonely an i just wanted t'see you an the wee lad – she smiled – brilliant – first time i was ever honest with her an she smiled – wanted t'bring the two a them out tonight for a meal – special dixie

y'know just the three of us – just spendin time together
talkin that's all – she wasn't keen on the idea – a smile
doesn't wipe the past out i understand that – the wee lad
says he wants t'go to the pictures – she says why don't you
take him – i'm takin my wee lad to the pictures tonight –
him an me – a boys' night out – ya could see it in his smile –
me an my da are goin to the pictures

PETESY. good – good – about this other thing

SOCRATES. what?

PETESY. the tiles

SOCRATES. aye everything's sound lunchtime

PETESY. a don't know – hearing about the plumber gettin
maclatched an that – it's thrown me a bit y'know

SOCRATES. fuck all t'do with us that's what ya said – ya said
that didn't ye?

PETESY. a know a know that – it's just maybe this is a bad
idea at the moment – maybe we should leave it for now
y'know – let the dust settle – give it a few days

SOCRATES. it's bein done now we decided that – no need for
any more thinkin about it

PETESY. i know what we decided – all i'm sayin is it might be
a bit dodgy

SOCRATES. she says to me in passin like that she was skint –
i've been givin her fuck all for a while y'know – i said til
her don't worry about that that's alright i'll get ye a chunk a
readies – it has t'be done – the woman has bills to pay an
shit – y'know

PETESY. leave it til monday or later next week even – now
seems like a bad time that's all

SOCRATES. i've already said – i've made a commitment here
y'know – i can't go back on that – she's happy about the
situation understand what i'm sayin

PETESY. i'm just not sure

SOCRATES. fuck not bein sure – ya put me in a corner earlier on – you were sure enough then

PETESY. put in fuck all corner – ya made yer own decision nothin else involved there – nothin

SOCRATES. you were on ma back an ya know it – made me feel like the wee girl's trip an everythin was beat out if i didn't come on board

PETESY. a business deal that's all – a don't wanna hear anything about that – a said t'ye an that's it

SOCRATES. ya gonna let me speak here – i've somethin t'say y'know

PETESY. don't be gettin all fuckin

SOCRATES. can i speak here? (*Pause.*) you had yer reasons – ya told me them – i understood the were important t'ye – so instead of tellin ye t'go an fuck yerself a came on board – all i'm doin now is the same thing – i'm tellin you this is important to me – it's not just doin somethin cause it's there t'be done – there's a reason an the readies are important to me

RANDOLPH *enters from on site.*

RANDOLPH. is there any chance

SOCRATES. we're talkin here randolph

RANDOLPH. a just wanted t'see if

SOCRATES. a don't give a fuck what ya want i've told ye we're talkin here – go in with ding-ding – whenever we're finished ya can do all the talkin ya want – go on – go

RANDOLPH *exits to other room.*

SOCRATES. ya understand what i'm sayin here – you asked me to do somethin an i went along with it – now i'm askin you to do something an i want you t'go along with it

PETESY. right

SOCRATES. right what?

PETESY. right right

SOCRATES. good – i'm just gonna nip out an get some
flowers – be a nice gesture that wouldn't it – a nice gesture

PETESY. be a nice gesture t'do some fuckin work – i think
that would be a nice gesture

SOCRATES. it's nearly lunchtime aren't ya only gonna sweep
up

PETESY. a was but if yer doin fuck all i'm doin fuck all

SOCRATES. whatever – i've a good feeling about today –
feels like the start a somethin – somethin different – a don't
know

SOCRATES *exits to on site.*

PETESY. fuck it

DING-DING *and* RANDOLPH *in other room.*

DING-DING. did ya count them then?

RANDOLPH. no

DING-DING. no

RANDOLPH. aye – no

DING-DING. why didn't ye count them?

RANDOLPH. ya never mentioned countin them

DING-DING. be a handy piece a information t'know

RANDOLPH. aye

DING-DING. i'll do it will a – seein it needs t'be done an you
didn't do it i do it

RANDOLPH. aye

DING-DING. might nip roun an see if a can get yer man about
the george formby dixie

RANDOLPH. what?

DING-DING. when i'm cleanin – forget it

RANDOLPH. aye

DING-DING *exits to on site.*

SOCRATES *enters from on site carrying a bunch of flowers.*

SOCRATES. smell them – fill yer snazzle with that aroma

PETESY. aye lovely

SOCRATES. from now on any job we're on all bring in a bunch of flowers – put them in vase chats leave'em about the place – instead a all this buildin concrete shite – bit a colour about the place

PETESY. aye

SOCRATES. i'm tellin ye – whenever ya feel a bit dankers an that have a butchers at the flowers – then go over an snort their beauty up intil yer napper – make ya feel at one with the universe – make ya feel glad to be alive boy

PETESY. ya reckon

SOCRATES. a do – what's the crack here – lunchtime – sit around for a few minutes – get them out t'fuck – go an do the business meet them roun for a swally

PETESY. aye

DING-DING *enters other room from on site.*

DING-DING. a hundred and forty four boxes – plenty – got that other chat sorted out too – wee man's happy enough – drop him roun the readies over the weekend – fucked he is – had a get him up outta his scratcher – no life for a person that – go in here chew the fat with these two get them outta the road do what we have t'do meet up with them later for a swally

RANDOLPH. aye

Work.

PETESY (*from the other room*). nose bag time

Lunchtime.

RANDOLPH *and* DING-DING *enter other room. There are four buckets turned upside down. They all sit and have tea from a flask – mid conversation.*

PETESY. that's what ya said – ya said that – didn't he say that – ya said everythin

DING-DING. ya did ya said everythin

SOCRATES. aye an what?

PETESY. no i'm not havin that – there must be some kind a dividin line some type a demarcation y'know

DING-DING. man's right cause somebody says somethin doesn't make it true – it's like yer man in the paper that geezer who put the dead sheep or somethin in that glass tank chat

PETESY. hearst

DING-DING. aye him – that's not art no matter what that fucker says t'me it's not art

SOCRATES. that's my point if ya accept any of it ya have t'accept the lot of it

RANDOLPH. that wall that we've tiled ship it over to the tate aye

SOCRATES. ya could aye why not

PETESY. right howl on here – say a person makes their own clothes

SOCRATES. that's art – do ya not think that's art

PETESY. ya gonna let me finish – ya never let anyone finish – a person makes their own clothes – the have t'wash them don't the – nobody wants glad rags art or otherwise that are fuckin abraham lincoln – the wash them an the put them on the line – no better still the wash them it's rainin outside so they hang them on the radiator t'dry – you go roun to their house t'visit an ye see the clothes dryin – is that an exhibition?

SOCRATES. clothes are meant t'be worn aren't the – anyway if the hang them for a purpose yes

PETESY. bollicks – and the were hung for a purpose – t'dry

DING-DING. socrates that purpose chat doesn't matter cause the person lookin at them doesn't know what the crack is

SOCRATES. what's that gotta do with it – it's the person who's hangin them not the one lookin at them

DING-DING. on the way roun to the house ya get soaked – ya take yer clothes off hang them beside the other ones – somebody else comes in has a jeff juke at the radiator – are yer clothes part of a exhibition now?

SOCRATES. i didn't make my clothes

DING-DING. same crack as before they don't know that

RANDOLPH (*to* PETESY). lend us yer cup

PETESY. no

SOCRATES (*to* DING-DING). what does that matter

DING-DING. petesy said it earlier on – art an all that fuckin gear has t'do with the geezer lookin at it not with the geezer who made it

PETESY. correct – thank you ding-ding

SOCRATES. it's one a them unanswerable ones like isn't it

PETESY. how's it unanswerable if we've answered it

RANDOLPH (*to* PETESY). you've finished yer tea lend us yer cup

PETESY. no – a keep tellin ya this – no

RANDOLPH. yer finished

PETESY. is he deaf – are you deaf

SOCRATES. give the wee lad the cup – fella's allowed a mouthful a tea

PETESY. no – he does this all the time no

RANDOLPH. do what all the time

PETESY. where's yer own cup

RANDOLPH. what ya askin that for – why's he askin that – a don't have a cup ya know a don't have a cup

SOCRATES. it's unanswerable – it is it's unanswerable

PETESY. me an ding-ding wouldn't be allowed t'get it right sure we wouldn't

DING-DING. we answer the unanswerable – that's us

RANDOLPH. am i invisible here

PETESY. might as well be yer not gettin the fuckin cup – this is my cup where's yer cup

RANDOLPH. i don't have a cup

SOCRATES. petesy just give him the fuckin cup

PETESY. give him yers

SOCRATES. i'm not finished yer finished give him the cup

PETESY. no – he has t'learn this is work he's responsible for his own stuff – not havin his own cup means he's not takin the thing seriously

SOCRATES. takin what seriously?

PETESY. work

SOCRATES. he doesn't take work seriously cause he doesn't bring a cup?

PETESY. not any cup his own cup – an yes

RANDOLPH. a don't want yer cup stick it

PETESY. a will

SOCRATES. i don't understan that – a cup like

PETESY. ya don't understand what?

SOCRATES. yer argument – the thinkin behind what yer sayin – it's all up the fuckin left

PETESY. what – there can't be logic t'normal things like – we can't have our own logic no – you only understand the logic of the loftier head firmly up yer jam roll world – we're not allowed logic

SOCRATES. settle yerself

PETESY. aye a know – but a mean it's not always up there some of it's down fuckin here y'know

DING-DING. ya can have my cup

RANDOLPH. yer cup?

PETESY (*to* DING-DING). yer gonna lend him yer cup?

SOCRATES. no one touches yer cup – it's a rule – we all thought the thing must've been handed down t'ye from moses

DING-DING (*to* RANDOLPH). do ya want a cup of tea or not?

RANDOLPH. aye but there's no way i'm usin yer cup – that's the cup – ya don't touch the cup even i know that – say a broke it – a don't want a lend of it no

DING-DING. i'm not lending ye it i'm givin ya it

SOCRATES. yer frightenin us ding-ding

PETESY. yer givin him yer cup the cup that no one can touch

DING-DING. when i first started a bought the cup – now i'm leavin might as well give it t'the wee lad

SOCRATES. yer passin him on a cup

RANDOLPH. yer passin me on a cup

DING-DING. aye

RANDOLPH. what am i gonna do with it?

DING-DING. drink yer fuckin tea out a it

RANDOLPH. no – that's serious shit that – like puttin a curse on me

DING-DING. it's only a cup

RANDOLPH. it's not it's the cup – it's ding-ding's cup – a workin man's cup – all that gear – couldn't drink outta that

DING-DING. suit yerself

SOCRATES. use mine

RANDOLPH. fill it up there (*To* PETESY.) what?

PETESY. no tea left

SOCRATES. time for a swally anyway

DING-DING. we headin roun aye

PETESY. aye

RANDOLPH. headin roun

Nobody moves.

DING-DING. sure petesy why don't you an socrates welt on roun there – we'll meet ye for a swally later

PETESY. meet us?

DING-DING. aye me an randolph has somethin t'sort out

PETESY. what?

DING-DING. what

PETESY. aye what?

DING-DING. what – funny as fuck sometimes the way ya just forget somethin when somebody asks ye – the head's a weird fuckin gadget like isn't it – randolph what is it – it's just not comin t'me – can you remember?

RANDOLPH. no

DING-DING. no?

RANDOLPH. no

PETESY. can't be too important can it

DING-DING. important alright – a have to – ah – have t'let the let the dog out – the dog has t'get out y'know

SOCRATES. what dog – you don't have a dog

DING-DING. a don't no that's right – the wee woman beside me though – wee woman beside me has a dog – she's away – i told here i'd do the business y'know – bring the wee lad with me y'know

SOCRATES. bring him – what for?

DING-DING. big fuckin dog – huge big fucker – take the two of us y'know – big beast of a thing

RANDOLPH. sure why don't me an petesy meet yous roun there – an socrates can go roun with ye let the dog out – socrates likes dogs

SOCRATES. i like dogs?

RANDOLPH. aye – yer always talkin about them aren't ya

SOCRATES. no – hate the fuckers hate all animals

RANDOLPH. i thought you like dogs – sure yous two go roun anyway – didn't ye want me for somethin petesy?

DING-DING. socrates can't go the dog'll do its nut

SOCRATES. i'm not goin anywhere – why would the dog do its nut?

DING-DING. funny fuckin animal

RANDOLPH. haven't me an you t'sort somethin out petesy – a tile slipped or somethin roun the other room?

PETESY. that's alright i sorted that out

SOCRATES. sure the dog wouldn't know me

DING-DING. that's it ya see hates people he doesn't know – anti social bastard

RANDOLPH. it's something else then it's not that – what is it petesy somethin else isn't it?

PETESY. no nothin else

SOCRATES. do you know the dog randolph?

RANDOLPH. what dog?

SOCRATES. the fuckin dog

RANDOLPH. no – are ya sure petesy?

PETESY. positive

RANDOLPH. right – that dog – ding-ding's dog – aye a know that one – big fuckin dog that – i'll go roun with ye ding-ding give ya a hand will a

DING-DING. yer comin roun t' help me with the dog?

RANDOLPH. oh aye

DING-DING. sure about that?

RANDOLPH. must be starvin by now

DING-DING. hank marvin – so we'll meet yous two roun there then

SOCRATES. aye

PETESY. aye

DING-DING. an what – are yous headin roun there now or what?

PETESY. hang on here for a while (*To* SOCRATES.) you wanna hang on here for a while?

SOCRATES. hang aroun for a while aye

DING-DING. welt roun now an get a seat for us all – don't wanna be standin fuck that caper – we don't wanna be standin

PETESY. place is empty it's always empty

DING-DING. aye that place that place is empty – we're not goin there goin roun the other place

SOCRATES. other place'll be bunged

DING-DING. that's why i'm sayin t'welt roun now an get a seat

PETESY. i'm not goin there – what would ya want t'go there for can't get movin in it – you hate that place anyway – always sayin it's full a shite hawks

DING-DING. a thought it be nice today – last day celebration – bit more up market y'know

PETESY. up market fuck that

SOCRATES. aye fuck that

DING-DING. what one do you wanna go to randolph?

RANDOLPH. the one ya need t'rush roun now an get a seat in

PETESY (*to* DING-DING). is that where you wanna go?

DING-DING. aye – be better – fuck that other place

PETESY. we'll go there then

DING-DING. yous better motor then – get a good seat one near the winda

SOCRATES. all the seats be away by now (*To* PETESY.) all be away by now

PETESY. long ago – ya couldn't get a seat in it now for love nor money

DING-DING. i'm tellin ye if ya welt roun ya will

PETESY. all gone now – we'll stand sure – i don't mind standin (*To* SOCRATES.) d'you mind standin?

SOCRATES. no – standin's alright

DING-DING. i'm not standin

PETESY. go to the normal place then

DING-DING. aye – other place is a fuckin kip anyway

SOCRATES. thought it was up market

DING-DING. it's a fuckin kip

PETESY. so we'll see yous roun there then – better pints anyway

RANDOLPH. yous headin now?

SOCRATES. too early

DING-DING. you'll miss the stew

PETESY. fuck the stew

SOCRATES. better get roun an sort that dog out – have its own leg chewed off by now

DING-DING. fuck the dog

SOCRATES. ya can't leave it with no grub

DING-DING. what d'you care sure you hate animals nature all that shite

SOCRATES. a know that but a wouldn't leave a dog with no grub

DING-DING. fuck the dog

PETESY. not goin roun then?

DING-DING. a just said fuck the dog – fuck the dog means i'm not goin roun

PETESY. the two a yous headin on roun then – roun to the other place

DING-DING. no

SOCRATES. you'll miss the stew

DING-DING. i don't like stew

SOCRATES. i've seen ye eat stew before

DING-DING. no ya haven't

SOCRATES. a have

PETESY. i've seen ye

RANDOLPH. so have i

DING-DING (to RANDOLPH). you've seen me eat stew have ye?

RANDOLPH. thought a did – must've been – soup – what was it soup?

DING-DING. aye soup – an that's shite roun there too

SOCRATES. food is shite roun there

PETESY. good pints though

RANDOLPH. the do – the do good pints

DING-DING. aye

PETESY. just sit here for a while then

DING-DING. looks like it

They sit in silence.

the notion for a gargle's wore off me

RANDOLPH. me too

DING-DING. if yous two wanna

PETESY. i'm not that keen myself

DING-DING. aye

They sit in silence.

DING-DING. ya sure now – i don't mind like – a know it's my leavin dixie an that but a mean if yous wanna welt on that's alright

PETESY. nah – a couldn't be arsed now

They sit in silence.

SOCRATES. fuck this – there's a problem here that needs t'be solved – honesty that's the thing – honesty

PETESY. socrates

SOCRATES. it's alright it's sound – my experience t'day has taught me that the only truth that the – that the best way forward in any situation is to open yerself up – to be honest

PETESY. sure about that?

SOCRATES. hundred percent – because of circumstances outside our normal work situation petesy and i have been forced into a situation we would not normally find ourselves in – the role of tea leafs – there's a pallet a tiles outside that we have planned to steal – i now realise that not lettin you two know our plans was a mistake – and i apologise as workmates and people we have known for some time – we should've treated you better and informed you of what we were plannin to do – which is what i am doin now (*Pause.*) so as this operation needs to be completed during lunch time petesy and i will now take our leave to do the dirty deed – unless of course you have something to say about the situation – in which case i would appreciate it if you would keep yer comments brief – as time is of the essence

PETESY (*applauding*). yer good – yer very good – i have something t'say

SOCRATES. you do?

PETESY. oh yes – where the fuck do you get off telling people my business – who the fuck give you permission t'speak on my behalf

SOCRATES. a thought

PETESY. ya didn't think – what ya did was open yer gob an speak – the one thing ya didn't do was fuckin think

DING-DING. may i intervene in this spirit of openness

PETESY. oh fuck aye intervene away

RANDOLPH. ding-ding i don't

DING-DING. i'm speakin for both of us – this situation involves us an what i'm doin is speakin for us – understan

PETESY. what?

DING-DING. me an the wee lad had planned t'steal the tiles too

PETESY. you an him?

DING-DING. didn't a just say that

SOCRATES. this is good – i like this – ya see now if we hadda been up front about this the situation

PETESY. shut up a minute

SOCRATES. i'm just sayin

PETESY. keep quiet – stop talkin a minute – you an him – when did you an him decide this?

DING-DING. what does that matter

PETESY. when?

DING-DING. this mornin – not that that's got fuck all t'do with you

> PETESY *hits* RANDOLPH. SOCRATES *and* DING-DING *restrain him.*

SOCRATES. what the fuck are ya at?

PETESY. let fuckin go of me let go

DING-DING. what ya hit him for he's a wee lad – what ya hit him for?

PETESY. i don't like being made a fucker of – let go a me let fuckin go

DING-DING. ya gonna calm down – get yer head clear here

PETESY. i'm calm – i'm sound – just let go

> *They let go.*

SOCRATES. ya sound?

PETESY. i'm sound

SOCRATES. you alright kid (*To* PETESY.) what the fuck you at

PETESY (*to* RANDOLPH). there was a problem ya should've fuckin said – stood up like a man an said face t'face – i'm there tryin a do the right thing by ye yer makin a fuckin eejit outta me – ya had somehin t'say ya should a fuckin said it – fucker ye

> RANDOLPH *lifts a hammer.*

DING-DING. put the hammer down – yer outta order – put the hammer down

PETESY. what ya gonna do with that – ya gonna use it

RANDOLPH. c'mon – c'mon – i'll put it through yer fuckin face

DING-DING. yer on yer own kid – there's rules y'know – there's rules – ya lift a hammer yer on yer own

RANDOLPH. fuck him

SOCRATES. we gonna calm down here a minute

PETESY. ya gonna use that – c'mon – ya wanna use it fuckin use it – c'mon

SOCRATES. calm down will ye

PETESY. fuck up nothin t'do with you so fuck up

SOCRATES. ya gonna start on me now

PETESY. if that's what ya want

SOCRATES. up t'yerself – ya wanna go that way we can go that way

RANDOLPH. ya can't treat me like shit – ya hear me – ya can't treat me like fuckin shit (*To* PETESY.) fuck you an the tiles – fuck you

DING-DING. what he got a do with you an the tiles?

RANDOLPH (*to* DING-DING). fuck you too – wanna grab me by the throat now – ya wanna have a go at that now do ye – fuck the two a yous

SOCRATES. what's goin on here?

RANDOLPH. the two a them – don't say that – don't say this – just me an you – just me an you – i'm stuck in the middle – doin me a favour – fuckin usin me

SOCRATES (*to* PETESY). you ask him?

PETESY (*to* RANDOLPH). ya had a spoke yer mind situation wouldn't a come up

DING-DING (*to* RANDOLPH). you agreed with him after ya agreed with me?

SOCRATES. you ask him?

PETESY. aye i asked him

RANDOLPH. he thinks yer fuckin crazy – that's why he asked me you can't be trusted yer fuckin crazy

SOCRATES. you say that?

DING-DING (*to* RANDOLPH). ya wee bastard ya ungrateful wee bastard

RANDOLPH. lookin after yer fuckin self that's what ya were doin

SOCRATES (*to* RANDOLPH). shut up – fuck you an fuck him (*To* PETESY.) did you say i was crazy?

PETESY. ya are fuckin crazy – talkin a lotta shite all the time – yer fuckin head's away with it

DING-DING (*to* SOCRATES). what you just say to me there?

SOCRATES (*to* DING-DING). fuck you you heard fuck you – i'm not interested in anythin to do with you alright – fuck you

DING-DING *grabs* SOCRATES *by the jumper.*

SOCRATES. get yer hand off me (*To* PETESY.) i was just tellin you how i felt what i was thinkin – i'm not crazy

PETESY. yer fuckin crazy

DING-DING (*to* SOCRATES). you don't talk to me like that

SOCRATES (*to* DING-DING). this is nothing to do with you – i'm warnin ye now get yer fuckin hand away from me

PETESY. yer fuckin crazy

SOCRATES (*grabs* PETESY *by the jumper*). say it one more time i'm gonna put yer head through the fuckin wall

PETESY (*grabs* SOCRATES *by the jumper*). any time yer ready fella – any fuckin time

SOCRATES *breaks free.*

SOCRATES. this is the wrong way t'go about this – we're goin t'do it we'll do it fuckin right (*Moves to* RANDOLPH.) put the hammer down – nobody's gonna touch ye just put the hammer down (*Shouts.*) put it down. (RANDOLPH *puts the hammer down.*) we right now – we ready t'go – i hate work – i hate bein here day in an day out with you fuckers – i hate talkin t'ye – i hate listenin t'ye – i hate bein in yer fuckin company – yous are ruinin my life an i fuckin hate yous for it

Silence.

PETESY. i don't like doin this

SOCRATES. you rather we went t'war?

PETESY (*to* SOCRATES). yer a whingin gurnin bastard – a wimp – a snivellin poncy cryin fucker – who makes the rest of us listen to the dribblin shite that pours outta yer thin lipped no backbone whingy wee fuckin mouth – i hate the sight of ye – i'm ashamed t'be in the same room as ye – you other two – yer just lazy bastards

Silence.

RANDOLPH. i – i

SOCRATES. go ahead

RANDOLPH. i look at you three an all a see are three no good slabberin fuckers who have done nothin with their lives – yous tell me what t'do an none of yous is worth spit – yous think yous are somethin an yes are nothing – just three fuckin tilers that have nothin – are goin nowhere – an lead empty fuckin lives

Silence.

SOCRATES. ding-ding (*Silence.*) ding-ding

DING-DING. i don't give a fuck about any of yous – yous mean nothin t'me – i've spent most a my time with yous an yous mean nothin t' me – i don't know who any of yous are (*He takes a hanky from his pocket and wipes his eyes.*)

SOCRATES. that it – we finished?

PETESY. looks like it

SOCRATES. it's been said – it's done – back t' normal now right

PETESY. ya think so

SOCRATES. has t'be – this is our livelihood we have t' work together it's as simple as that

DING-DING. it's my last day

SOCRATES. have you somethin t'say about that?

DING-DING. no

SOCRATES. that's it finished then

DING-DING. finished

They all sit. Silence.

that united's a shower of jammie bastards aren't the

PETESY. they've the referees bribed and everything for fuck sake

SOCRATES. stop talkin nonsense

DING-DING. certainly the have

RANDOLPH. i think the have

Work. It's nearly the end of the day.

Both rooms are tiled and cleaned. The pallet of tiles is now on stage. PETESY *and* SOCRATES *enter from on site carrying two boxes of tiles each. They set them with the others.*

SOCRATES. this is fuckin stupid – we should've just fired them in the van

PETESY. they're better here – after work when the site's empty then we'll fire them in the van

SOCRATES. i can't be hangin about here – ya understan that – do whatever we have t'do an shoot the crow

PETESY. it'll take as long as it takes

SOCRATES. can't be late for the wee lad this pictures thing's important – can't be late – don't wanna be messin the wee lad about – wanna show him i'm dependable – don't want him goin through life thinkin i'm lettin him down all the time – that's all i'm sayin

PETESY. i wanna get home to y'know – sort this shit out then a can tell the wee girl i've got the readies for her for france – a wanna do that – i don't wanna be hangin aroun either

SOCRATES. ya get the readies t'night – if ya get it t'night i can give it t'her t'night – wee lad to the pictures give her the readies – it would help create a nice type of a feelin about the place y'know

PETESY. t'night's difficult – t'morrow

SOCRATES. t'morrow?

PETESY. aye – jimmy blow be on the gargle t'night – ya not get him have t'be t'morrow

SOCRATES. positive now – a can tell her it's on its way

PETESY. aye tell her

SOCRATES. ya sure?

PETESY. a fuckin said didn't a – didn't a just say it

SOCRATES. right – know what the wee lad wants t'see – i thought this was fuckin brilliant

PETESY. what?

SOCRATES. thunderbirds – when i was a kid i lived breathed and shite that show – anything he wants t'know he just has t'ask his da – thunderbirds was the business – thunderbirds are go – only one a didn't reckon was number five – know that chat up in space – that wee lad never got home – i always felt that was a bit outta order

PETESY. did the not shift him aroun – i thought the did – the did the shifted him aroun – a few episodes in space then back t'the island for a rest – cuppla gargles scratch his cleavers beside the pool

SOCRATES. alan ya called him

PETESY. aye

SOCRATES. ya reckon he got shore leave?

PETESY. certainly he did

SOCRATES. might a done alright – makes sense like doesn't
it – go gaga in space on yer lonesome

PETESY. aye

SOCRATES. could never work out that wee girl – know the
wee ethnic minority chat – couldn't work out what the fuck
she was at

PETESY. she was the maid – wasn't she the maid – aye she
was the maid

SOCRATES. maid – the had a fuckin maid?

PETESY. aye – she was always carryin gargle aroun on trays
wasn't she – i always thought she was the maid

SOCRATES. adopted daughter maybe – could a been both

PETESY. how the fuck could she have been both – she was a
skivvy – the treated her like a skivvy that means she was on
the payroll – you adopt someone ya don't treat them like a
skivvy do ye

SOCRATES. that's true

PETESY. i never liked that show anyway – joe ninety was a
better show

SOCRATES. get t'fuck – lady penelope parker that big pink
fuckin roller – behave yerself

PETESY. joe ninety

SOCRATES. away an fuck – joe ninety – puttin them dopey
testicles on him

PETESY. couldn't've been any dopier than the ones brains
wore – the had special powers those blue chats had special
powers – once he put them on an got into that other chat

that spinnin cage message ya knew the world was a safe place – nobody fucked with joe ninety – wee lad used t'eat dynamite for fuck sake

SOCRATES. guff – fuckin nazi he was

PETESY. who?

SOCRATES. blonde hair blue eyes an his granny was a german or somethin – fuckin nazi

PETESY. behave yerself

SOCRATES. alright mightn't been a nazi but he was definitely gay – never once saw him with a wee girl – not once

PETESY. he was only a kid what ya talkin about gay – wee lad was savin the world no time for that sexual chat anyway – thunderbirds heap a shite

SOCRATES. doesn't matter t'me one way or the other just good t'be takin the wee lad out that's all

RANDOLPH *enters carrying two boxes of tiles. Puts them with the rest.*

SOCRATES (*to* RANDOLPH). he thinks joe ninety's better than thunderbirds

RANDOLPH. what's he talkin about?

PETESY. nothin – shootin the shit – passin the time – nothin – that the last a them?

RANDOLPH. aye

SOCRATES. joe ninety – yer fuckin head's away with it

PETESY (*to* RANDOLPH). ya sure now – none lyin about out there ya checked?

RANDOLPH. none lyin about – a checked – that's the last of them

SOCRATES (*looking at tiles*). doesn't look like much does it

PETESY. looks like a pallet a tiles – what ya want it t'look like

SOCRATES. i know it looks like a pallet a tiles – that's cause it is a pallet a tiles

PETESY. einstein

SOCRATES. i mean the bit a hassle an that it caused – doesn't look like much like

PETESY. look better if there were more a them that's true

RANDOLPH. doesn't matter what it looks like – gettin us what we want isn't it

PETESY. shouldn't have t'fuckin steal t'get what ya want though should ye

SOCRATES. where's ding-ding?

RANDOLPH. way roun t'buy a bucket

PETESY. bucket a what?

RANDOLPH. winda cleanin – a winda cleaner's bucket

PETESY (*to* SOCRATES). that's what we've t'work with (*To* RANDOLPH.) what the fuck are you talkin about?

RANDOLPH. did he not say to ye?

PETESY. if he said would we be askin

RANDOLPH. a thought he said t'ye when we all agreed about the tiles an that – did he not say?

PETESY. he didn't say

RANDOLPH. that's what he's doin with his share of the poppy

SOCRATES. buyin buckets?

RANDOLPH. winda cleanin – some oul lad he knows sellin his round – ding-ding's buyin it off him

SOCRATES. aye

RANDOLPH. i'm tellin ye that's what he said – reckons it's gonna stop him from dyin or somethin

SOCRATES. winda cleanin stop him from dyin

RANDOLPH. somethin like that

SOCRATES. winda cleanin

RANDOLPH. i'm only tellin ye what the man said – i don't know maybe he reckons winda cleaners don't die or somethin – i don't know

PETESY. fair play til him

SOCRATES. yer right – fair play til him's right – winda cleanin wouldn't be my preferred occupation – good luck til him though

RANDOLPH. somethin wrong with his head

SOCRATES. nothin wrong with his head – man's allowed t'work on – wants t'do that that's up t'himself – oh no he's allowed t'do that

PETESY. man's showin a bit a enterprise isn't he – nobody tellin him what t'do – out on his own – that's alright – that's sound

DING-DING *enters from on site carrying a bucket.*

SOCRATES. fuck it's george formby

PETESY. when i'm cleaning dixies ding-ding wha – i've an oul shammie an a string vest in the house – that type a object would be of use t'ya now a imagine

DING-DING (*to* RANDOLPH). that was nobody's business – ya understan – you do too much talkin wee lad

RANDOLPH. i thought you'd already said i didn't know

SOCRATES. no now ding-ding that not right don't be blamin the wee lad here – we're allowed t'know that now c'mon til

PETESY. if ya were gonna say nothin how were ya gonna explain the bucket?

DING-DING. explain what it's just a bucket

PETESY. ya buy them all the time do ye

DING-DING. if ya had a asked me about the bucket i'd've told ye to fuck off

PETESY. that's lovely talk that from a winda cleaner – can ya picture him half way up the ladder some wee woman says t'him want yer bucket filled mister – away an fuck yerself

SOCRATES. ya can't be at that now ding-ding – when yer a winda cleaner ya can't be talkin like a tiler

DING-DING. away an fuck yerself

PETESY *and* SOCRATES *laugh, then* RANDOLPH *and eventually* DING-DING.

SOCRATES. what was that

PETESY. that's tiler speak for thank you for expressing your opinion but on this occasion i feel i must beg to differ

PETESY *and* SOCRATES *laugh harder.*

SOCRATES/PETESY. away an fuck yerself

PETESY. member the day we were standin in the kitchen wee woman says t'him (DING-DING.) do you think (*Laughter.*) do you think the patterns should be randomised or uniform – how the fuck would i know

They are all in a giggling fit.

SOCRATES. wee woman says – i don't think there's any need for that language

SOCRATES/PETESY. away an fuck yerself

DING-DING. oh aye very good aye a know

PETESY. the other one – the white or the blue tiles – up t'yerself dear – you are the tiler – am i fuck

SOCRATES. what about – attention

DING-DING. member that – she had lost it – something not right with that wee woman's napper

RANDOLPH. what – what was that?

PETESY. you not with us then no

SOCRATES. no – sure it must've been a good two years ago – wee woman we were workin for had the hots for him (DING-DING) – definitely some type a sexual thing goin on

DING-DING. that's not right now – don't listen t'him – that's not right

PETESY. didn't she keep givin ya apples

DING-DING. she wasn't right in the napper that's why

PETESY. she didn't give me an him any

SOCRATES. she did not

PETESY. she says to us – what's wrong with yer friend he
doesn't smile a lot is he unhappy – socrates says til her (*To*
SOCRATES.) what was it shrapnel – a bullet?

SOCRATES. no a metal plate in his head

PETESY. aye – he says that ding-ding suffered some serious
shit durin the war an he had t'get a metal plate in his head
which was fuckin him up

SOCRATES. no – i said t'her that yer head was divided into a
happy part an a sad part an the plate was stoppin the blood
gettin t'his happy part – wee woman was away with the
fairies like – this got her talkin about the war an she was
askin what battalion ding-ding was in

RANDOLPH. you in the war?

DING-DING. no – fuck

SOCRATES. askin a whole lotta stuff – so me an him made it
up – group squadron fuck i don't know whatever it was –
she was really gettin into it – she was in the army an all
(*Starts giggling.*)

PETESY. she left right – it was near lunchtime – we're in the
bathroom or somethin (DING-DING's *giggling.*) talkin
away – bullshit – waitin on lunch – she bursts in the door an
she had all the gear on her – her army uniform y'know –
(*Laughing.*) – fuck – she had an apple in her hand for ding-
ding – fuck – she shouted out attention here's an apple for
you soldier – we're all lookin at her didn't know what t'say –
lookin at ding-ding – an apple for ya soldier – he says put it
on the plate (*Laughter.*) she salutes marches over an puts
the apple on his head

Mobile phone rings. PETESY *answers it.*

SOCRATES. william fuckin tell

DING-DING. attention soldier

PETESY (*on phone*). yes john how are ya – no no – just a bit
of a laugh – aye oul story – all red up aye just about to –
aye – what – but ya can't – a know – john ya can't expect –
no – i understand that – there's no need for – right –
i understand that but jesus john y'know – no i'm not – no
i'm not saying that – right – right – that's extra – yes aye –
it'll be – finished yes – he's here do ye wanna – no right –
aye right (*Phone down.*)

RANDOLPH. attention

PETESY. fuck up

SOCRATES. what?

> PETESY *walks to tiles puts his hand under the pallet and
> take out a delivery note and hands it to* SOCRATES.

deliver note – an what?

PETESY. ya not fuckin read – the tiles are on it – can ya not
see that – it's fuckin plain enough isn't it

SOCRATES. the tiles are on it?

PETESY. randolph go out to the van an get the tool box back in

SOCRATES. for what – what ya need the tool box for?

PETESY. to work – what d'ya normally fuckin need it for

SOCRATES. we're finished

PETESY. the tiles are for here – there's another room t'be done
an it's t'be done t'night (*To* RANDOLPH.) did i tell you
t'go an do somethin – well go an fuckin do it

> RANDOLPH *exits to on site.*

SOCRATES. i don't get this – a don't understan

PETESY. simple enough – we've more fuckin work t'do an
we're gonna fuckin do it – what the fuck don't ya
understand about that

SOCRATES. ya didn't say anything to him why didn't ye say
anything to him?

PETESY. like what?

DING-DING. what room?

PETESY. what room what?

DING-DING. what room we workin in?

PETESY. room – one down the bottom a the corridor

SOCRATES. ya should've said somethin

   DING-DING *lifts two boxes of tiles and exits to on site.*

PETESY. we're doin it – what else is there to say

SOCRATES. tell him no

PETESY. he'll get another squad in – that's us out

SOCRATES. fat bastard – he can't do that – fuck'im

PETESY. he's done it – there is no he can't do that – he's fuckin done it

SOCRATES. you should've said somethin

PETESY. don't say that again – there was fuck all i could say – ya understan – fuck all

   RANDOLPH *enters with tool box.*

   other room

   RANDOLPH *exits to on site.*

SOCRATES. all night?

PETESY. four or five hours i'd say

SOCRATES. that's it like – ya make plans – have other business in the world t'sort out – all of that means fuck all though – work fucks all that up – yer told what t'do an ya do it

PETESY. it's no different for me socrates i had plans too

SOCRATES. fuck'im

PETESY. correct

SOCRATES. four t'five hours?

PETESY. aye

SOCRATES. positive?

PETESY. aye

SOCRATES. have t'let the wee lad down – try t'make amends now i've t'fuckin let him down again

PETESY. better start bringin these roun here – sooner we start sooner we're finished

They lift two boxes of tiles each. Exiting to on site.
SOCRATES *stops. He puts the tiles back.*

SOCRATES. i am finished

RANDOLPH *enters from on site.*

i'm not doin it – i've made my mind up – i'm not doin it

PETESY. don't start socrates just lift the fuckin things an c'mon

SOCRATES. no

PETESY. i'm tired i wanna get t'fuck outta here – can we just get this finished

SOCRATES. no – there's more important things in the world than this – i'm bringin the wee lad to the pictures – mightn't seem like much – mightn't seem important but that's what i'm doin

PETESY. yer just gonna fuck off an leave the rest of us – doesn't matter that it'll take us twice as long or fuck all – just you like worry about gettin yer world sorted out an fuck the rest of us

SOCRATES. you can do what ya want

PETESY. no i can't – i've responsibilities – i need work i need t'earn – that's what a have t'fuckin do – there's no choice here

SOCRATES. i'm bringin the wee lad to the pictures

PETESY. i'm not coverin for ya – do whatever ya like but i'm not coverin for ye – an if heavy hole asks me i'm tellin him the truth – ya fucked off – he'll sack ye ya know that

SOCRATES. you do what ya have t'do that's yer business – i'm just tellin ye what i'm doin (*Puts his coat on and lifts the flowers.*)

PETESY. i'm not coverin for ye

SOCRATES. i'll maybe see ya on monday

SOCRATES *exits on site.*

PETESY. you'll not be here on fuckin monday – queuing up at the fuckin brew without a pot t'piss in that's where you'll be (*Pause.*) bastard

RANDOLPH. what we doin about his overtime?

PETESY. what?

RANDOLPH. we could all do with the extra readies an if we're doin his work we should split the readies he was goin' t'get – fuck'im – we've earned it he hasn't

PETESY. he gets whatever's due t'him for t'night plus we cover for him – an if heavy hole asks anythin he went home sick

RANDOLPH. but you just said

PETESY. doesn't matter what the fuck i said – that's between me an him – all you need to know is we're coverin for him an that's it

RANDOLPH. why?

PETESY. you know fuck all do ye – why – cause the fella's right that's why – he's doin the right thing

RANDOLPH. that's not right

PETESY. that's what's happenin

RANDOLPH. i'm not doin it

PETESY (*up close to* RANDOLPH). you do what i tell you t'fuckin do – an don't think i've forgotten what ya said earlier cause i haven't – goin nowhere – that what ya think – i'll tell ya somethin kid yer gonna be the exact fuckin same – start bringin the tiles down to the other room

RANDOLPH *lifts two boxes of tiles and exits on site.*

PETESY (*on mobile phone*). i'm gonna be late – i just am
that's why – i'm workin

Late evening.

Empty wooden pallet on stage. RANDOLPH *is sitting on
pallet drinking tea and flicking through his magazine.*
DING-DING *sleeping.*

RANDOLPH. what d'ya think ding-ding red or black – i think
black myself – there's somethin classy about a black
number – what ya reckon – how the fuck do you do that one
minute yer talkin next yer dead to the world – a big black
one that's what i reckon – wanna hear the shit i'd to take
from petesy there – fuck'im – no mention a the job either –
that's that banjaxed – fuck'im – all a did was speak my
mind like – that was the crack like wasn't it – be like the
rest of yous – i don't think so – save the readies get the bike
i'm away. (*Accidentally knocks his tea over.*) fuck that –
i was enjoyin that – have a wee sip of yers ding-ding wha –
you just sleep away there (*He drinks from* DING-DING*'s
cup.*) better sayin fuck all like aren't ye – just keep yer nose
down an say fuck all – he's gonna give me a lotta shit like
now – fuck'im – i'm goin roun t'morrow an joinin that
bikin club effort – drop them a few shillin's – tenner or
somethin that'll get the ball rollin – pity there wasn't a
winda cleanin club goin ya could have a crack at that ding-
ding – it's fucked that like innit – thinkin yer gettin
somethin an endin up with fuck all – what about blue – aye
blue be alright wouldn't it

PETESY (*off stage*). randolph c'mon til

RANDOLPH. right – might say t'him about the job – aye –
leave the bikin club thing until he gives me the wire about
the job – fuck'im – c'mon ding-ding son – sooner we get
this finished sooner we get home

RANDOLPH *nudges* DING-DING. DING-DING *slumps
over. He is dead.*